Clouds, Rain, and Snow

Dean Galiano

the rosen publishing group's
rosen central
new york

Published in 2000 by The Rosen Publishing Group, Inc.
29 East 21st Street, New York, NY 10010

First Edition

Galiano, Dean.
    Clouds, rain, and snow / Dean Galiano.
        p.   cm. -- (Weather watchers' library)
    Includes bibliographical references and index.
    Summary: Surveys cloud dynamics and formation and the
process by which rain and snow develop to become precipitation.
    ISBN 0-8239-3092-0
    1. Cloud physics Juvenile literature. 2. Rain and rainfall
Juvenile literature. 3. Snow Juvenile literature. [1.
clouds. 2.
    Rain and rainfall. 3. Snow.] I. title. II. Series.
    QC921.5.G35 1999
    551.57'6--dc21   99-29972
                                                            CIP

Manufactured in the United States of America

CONTENTS

Introduction 4

1 Clouds 7

2 Rain 23

3 Snow 31

Glossary 42

For Further Reading 44

Resources 45

Index 46

Introduction

Everyone seems to have an interest in the weather—and why not? After all, weather affects each of us every day. We often plan our lives around the weather. On warm, sunny days most of us put on our summer clothes and enjoy being outside. Sometimes when it's raining we decide to stay in all day. Whole weekends are sometimes made or ruined by the weather. Who wants to go swimming at the beach if it's cold and cloudy? Even the prices of the food we eat are affected by weather.

All of the weather that we experience takes place in something called the atmosphere. The atmosphere is a thin layer of air that surrounds Earth. When you look up into the huge sky, with its great masses of floating clouds, it is hard to think of the atmosphere as being small. But it really is. Weather actually happens in a very limited space. If Earth were shrunk to the size of a basketball, our atmosphere would be thinner than a piece of notebook paper!

We have all looked up and seen the clouds in the sky. And most of us know that clouds are where precipitation (any kind of water that falls to Earth's surface, such as rain, snow, hail, or sleet) comes from. But have you ever wondered where the clouds themselves come from? What are they made of? How can they float in the sky filled with the same water that we drink, bathe in, and water our plants with?

Clouds add to the beauty of nature.

1 Clouds

On most days when we look up into the sky, we will see clouds. They come in all shapes and sizes. Usually the clouds that we see are white and puffy. You may have gazed up at these clouds on such days, recognizing common shapes in their forms. There are also thin, wispy clouds that seem to be on the verge of disappearing into the wind. And then there are the large, dark clouds that give birth to thunderstorms.

Even though these kinds of clouds all look different from one another, they are all made up of the same thing: water vapor. Water vapor is actually water in the form of a gas. Being a gas, it is made up of millions of tiny particles that float in the air. This is different from the liquid form of water. It is also different from ice, the solid form of water.

Clouds like the ones floating above this farm are actually made of water.

Photographed from space, the Earth shows its variety of cloud and weather formations.

The air surrounding Earth is called the atmosphere. It is made up of gases such as nitrogen, oxygen, carbon dioxide, and (most important to the weather) water vapor. All together the atmosphere weighs nearly 6 quadrillion tons. One quadrillion equals one thousand billion. Of this total, water vapor accounts for only about 2 percent. But its role in creating the weather that we experience every day is more important than all of the other gases put together.

The reason that water vapor is so important in the weather process is that it has the ability to absorb heat. Heat is a form of energy. Because water vapor can absorb heat, it is able to store energy. This energy, along with moisture, is responsible for much of the weather we experience. This includes thunderstorms, with their wind and rain.

Clouds from the Sea

Most of the water vapor found in the atmosphere comes from the ocean. Although we cannot see it, water is continually moving from the ocean into the atmosphere. This process is called evaporation. Water molecules are always breaking loose from the surface of the ocean and moving into the air. If you boil a pot of water you can actually see evaporation taking place. Boiling water evaporates in the form of steam. The warmer the water is, the quicker it will evaporate. Since the ocean is much cooler than a pot of boiling water, the evaporation is much slower, and therefore cannot be seen.

Evaporation happens because water molecules have something called kinetic energy. Kinetic energy is the energy of things in motion. The fact that water is always moving allows water molecules to break loose from the surface of oceans, lakes, rivers, and any other body of water, no matter how large or small. The puddles you see after a rainstorm dry up quickly under the heat of the sun. They are also evaporating, and the water in them goes back up into the air.

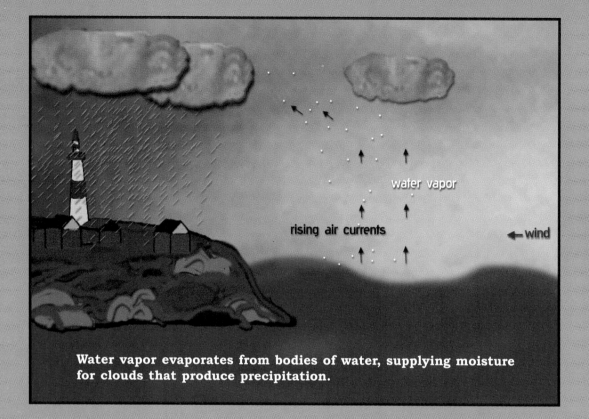

water vapor

rising air currents

←wind

Water vapor evaporates from bodies of water, supplying moisture for clouds that produce precipitation.

As water molecules enter the air, they add to the amount of moisture in the atmosphere. As we can see from boiling water, water molecules will evaporate more quickly from warm water than from cold water. Also, water molecules can more easily break free into warmer air than into colder air. For these two reasons, the greatest amount of water enters the atmosphere from warm, tropical oceans.

Condensation

Water vapor is always present in the air. However,

there are many hours and even days throughout the year that are cloudless and without precipitation. In regions where the humidity—the amount of water vapor in the air—is very low, such as over deserts, nearly every day of the year is sunny. By contrast, regions of high humidity, such as tropical rain forests, have very few cloudless days.

Desert regions (left) are mostly dry, with little chance for condensation to occur, resulting in few clouds and little rain. Very humid, tropical regions (above) produce plenty of condensation, which creates clouds and rain.

CONDENSATION EXPERIMENT:

You can actually watch condensation happen by taking a glass of ice water outside on a humid summer day. In just a few minutes, water droplets will form on the outside of the glass.

The glass of ice water allows the two conditions of water vapor condensation to happen: First it cools the air to the dew point (the temperature at which water vapor will condense into liquid water); and, second, the glass provides an object for water vapor to collect on.

What causes clouds to form? Clouds are made up of liquid water droplets. The process by which these droplets form is called condensation. For water vapor to condense into water, two conditions must exist:

⊙ The air temperature must cool to a certain point. This temperature is called the dew point.

⊙ The air must contain objects of some kind—usually dust, salt, or other tiny particles—that the water vapor can cling to. These objects are called condensation nuclei.

Even in places such as deserts, where humidity is low and rain is relatively light, condensation can take place and clouds can form. This is because the air over such places, although relatively dry, still holds a large amount of moisture. If the temperature reaches the dew point, and the air contains enough condensation nuclei, condensation will occur.

In addition to producing clouds, condensation is what causes dew to form. Because temperatures usually drop at night, we see dew on the ground in the mornings.

Cloud Formation

Much of the moisture that appears as clouds over the United States comes from the Atlantic and Pacific Oceans, as well as from the Gulf of Mexico. The clouds you see overhead may have traveled hundreds, or even thousands, of miles. Often the moisture itself may have traveled this far before it cooled enough to form clouds.

In the Earth's atmosphere, dust particles and sea salts make up most of the condensation nuclei. If it were not for these tiny particles in the air, water vapor could not condense into clouds. Experiments have proven that moist air cleaned of all condensation nuclei, such as dust or sea salts, will fail to condense even when it has been completely saturated with water vapor. Yet when dust or smoke particles, from a smoldering match, for example, are added to the moist air, condensation will quickly occur.

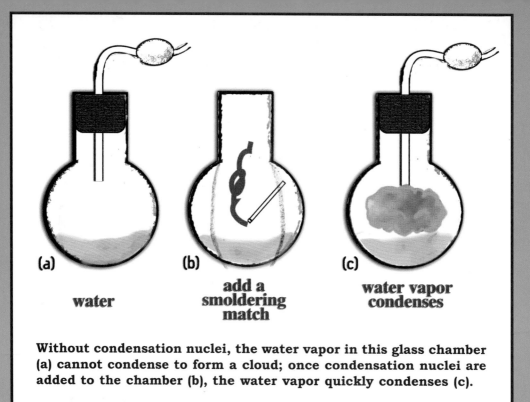

(a)
water

(b)
add a
smoldering
match

(c)
water vapor
condenses

Without condensation nuclei, the water vapor in this glass chamber (a) cannot condense to form a cloud; once condensation nuclei are added to the chamber (b), the water vapor quickly condenses (c).

The most important condensation nuclei in Earth's atmosphere are sea salts. Salt particles are thrown into the air as part of sea spray. Large amounts of sea salt are sprayed into the air by waves breaking on the ocean shore and from white-capped waves at sea. These tiny particles of sea salt are lifted upward by air movements and are transported great distances. Sea salts, as well as smoke and dust particles, are very likely to attract water. The billions of salt particles drifting around in the atmosphere, along with billions of tons of water evaporated from the sea, will quickly combine to

The fine spray caused by crashing waves is easily pulled into the atmosphere by winds. The salt particles contained in this spray act as condensation nuclei.

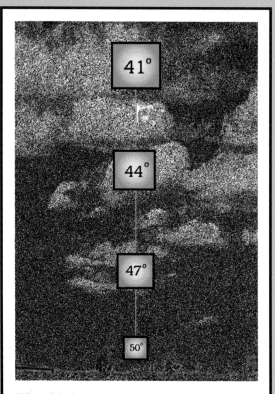

41°

44°

47°

50°

The higher an air mass rises, the cooler it becomes. When the dew point is reached, condensation, and thus clouds, appear.

form clouds when the air temperature cools to the dew point.

Air may be cooled in a number of ways. The most important cooling process in the formation of clouds is called expansion. Expansion results when masses of air move upward in the atmosphere. As a mass of air moves upward, it moves into regions of thinner air and lower air pressure. Air pressure is also called atmospheric pressure. This is the force at which one air mass presses against another air mass. The mass of rising air then expands, or spreads outward, under its own pressure. As it expands, it also cools as the air molecules move farther apart from each other. When the expanding air cools enough to reach the dew point, the water vapor in the air collects on condensation nuclei and forms cloud droplets, which form clouds.

Types of Clouds

Although clouds seem to have many different shapes, most fit into one of three basic categories: cumuliform (puffy clouds), stratiform (flat clouds), and cirrus (ice clouds).

Cumuliform Clouds

The way clouds look indicates the types of air movements taking place in the atmosphere. Cumulus clouds—a type of cumuliform cloud—often appear as white, puffy masses scattered across the sky. They indicate the presence of invisible columns of warm, moist air swirling rapidly upward from the ground. Cumulus clouds generally form at 3,000 to 4,000 feet above the ground. The bottoms of these

Cumulus clouds are a type of cumuliform cloud.

clouds indicate where the dew point was reached. The force that drives the air upward is usually caused by the unequal heating of different parts of the land by the sun. Cumuliform clouds are also created when masses of warm, moist air are forced upward by masses of cool, dry air. This happens, for example, when warm, moist air masses from the Gulf of Mexico meet cool, dry air masses from Canada. Since the warm, moist air mass is lighter than the cool, dry air mass, it is lifted up. When it reaches the dew point, clouds begin to form.

In good or fair weather, cumulus clouds tend to stay small. They are usually only about a mile tall. This is because as each cloud extends upward, it runs into dry air that mixes with the cloud. This causes the water droplets that make up the cloud to evaporate and keeps the cloud from stretching any higher into the atmosphere. However, some-times very warm, moist air swirls up through the cloud column, causing changes to take place. The air begins to rise faster, sometimes extending into a part of the atmosphere called the stratosphere, seven miles up or higher. Such clouds, called cumulonimbus, usually produce storms. These clouds are often referred to as thunderheads. Thunderheads are gray or dark gray puffy clouds.

Stratiform Clouds

Stratiform clouds take the shape of a sheet-like mass, as if a fog were lifted up off the ground. These clouds are classified as low clouds, usually starting at 6,000 feet. Stratiform clouds are often formed when moist, tropical air masses are lifted slowly as they pass over cooler, drier air masses. A common type of stratiform cloud is called a stratus cloud. If you have ever looked up into the sky on a drizzly morning and seen the sky totally gray, you have seen a stratus cloud. Gray, drizzly mornings are typical of stratus clouds.

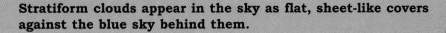

Stratiform clouds appear in the sky as flat, sheet-like covers against the blue sky behind them.

Cirrus Clouds

Cirrus clouds are thin, feathery clouds that are always found at great heights in the atmosphere, usually above 20,000 feet. These bright white clouds are made up of ice crystals. The trails formed by high-flying jets are similar to these clouds. Like cirrus clouds, these jet trails are made up of ice crystals. The ice crystals in cirrus clouds are produced when water vapor freezes as it hits the very cold air of high altitudes.

Cirrus clouds scattered across the sky indicate fair weather. If they are moving across the sky as a thin sheet and the sheet begins to thicken, they signal stormy weather.

Strange Cloud

Cumuliform, stratiform, and cirrus clouds are common because the types of weather conditions that form them happen often. Some kinds of clouds, however, only form in certain areas and under certain conditions. One type of unusual cloud, called altocumulus (high cumulus) lenticularis (lens-shaped), actually looks like a flying saucer. These clouds form near mountain ranges. The high mountains disturb the atmosphere's normal air flow, creating this UFO-like effect in the cloud shapes.

The hot jet-engine exhaust quickly condenses into ice crystals at high altitudes, resembling cirrus clouds.

Umbrellas keep us dry during rainstorms, but the water is essential to our survival.

2 Rain

After water has evaporated from Earth's surface, it may return to the ground as precipitation—rain, sleet, hail, or snow. Every day large quantities of water evaporate and move into the air. The moisture-filled air condenses into clouds, and the clouds release their moisture in the form of rain or snow. The water is then absorbed into the ground and eventually flows back into the sea, where it will evaporate again. This process is called the water cycle, and it happens around us all the time.

We depend on the water cycle to live. If there were no rainfall, plants and trees would dry up and die. Farmers would not be able to grow the crops needed to feed us, and the animals that we depend on for food would not be able to survive.

The "Dust Bowl" that affected the Great Plains is an example of the disastrous effects of the interruption of the water cycle. In the 1930s, a series of

Topsoil carried away during the "Dust Bowl" droughts in the 1930s is an example of what happens when the water cycle is interrupted.

droughts—extended periods where little or no rain fell—struck the Great Plains, causing the crops to dry up and die. The dry soil lay exposed to the wind. The winds lifted up the soil and carried it. Huge clouds of dust, which could be seen from hundreds of miles away, filled and darkened the air. Ten years went by before the land could be farmed again, because the fertile soil had been blown away.

Cloud Droplets and Raindrops

Precipitation depends on cloud formation. All clouds are made up of cloud droplets. The size of the droplets depends upon the size and type of cloud. Cumulus clouds tend to contain larger droplets than stratus clouds because they are thicker clouds that have higher bases. In a typical small cumulus cloud, cloud droplets are usually less than 50 microns (0.002 inches) across. This is so small that it cannot be seen with the naked eye. In large cumulus clouds, droplets are usually over 50 microns across. By contrast, typical cloud droplets in stratus clouds are much smaller than those in cumulus clouds, and therefore the shape of the cloud is different.

Cloud droplets are held up in the air by upcurrents—winds blowing upward from beneath the clouds. Raindrops are formed when cloud droplets combine together and become too heavy to be held up by the upcurrents within the cloud. Although cloud droplets are

Raindrops come in many sizes.

all very small—it takes millions of them to form one raindrop—some are larger than others. The larger a cloud droplet is, the faster it will fall through the cloud. As large cloud droplets collide with slower-falling small droplets, they combine to form even larger droplets. As the droplets combine, they increase in size and are able to collect even more droplets. If the falling droplet is inside a thick cloud, such as a cumulus cloud, it may gather

Acid Rain

Pollution collected in the atmosphere by automobile exhaust and factory chimneys has caused a serious problem known as acid rain. Cloud droplets and raindrops are naturally slightly acidic. But acid from pollution has raised their acidity to a dangerous level. In parts of the United States where major factories are located, acid rain has damaged the trees in many forests. When acid rain mixes with the water in rivers and lakes, it can also kill large numbers of fish.

The United States is not the only country suffering from this problem. Many European nations are experiencing similar problems with acid rain. One of the world's most famous forests—the Black Forest, in Germany—has been damaged by the harmful effects of acid rain.

Factory smokestacks send tons of waste into the air each year that returns to the ground as acid rain.

enough droplets to form a raindrop that is heavy enough to fall to Earth.

Ice crystals also play a role in producing raindrops. In the upper parts of thick cumulus clouds, the temperatures are cooler than in the lower parts. The water droplets in the lower parts of the cloud are liquid. But as they are lifted by winds into the upper parts of the cloud, they freeze and form ice crystals. The ice crystals then act as condensation nuclei, just as sea salts and dust particles do. They attract water vapor from other water droplets and grow larger. As the ice crystals grow larger, they become heavier and begin to fall through the cloud. As they fall, they bump into and combine with other ice crystals and water droplets and become even larger. Soon they grow too large and heavy to be supported by the upcurrents within the cloud, and they fall toward Earth. As they fall through the atmosphere, they meet with higher temperatures and begin to melt. By the time they hit the ground, they have melted into raindrops.

Shapes of Raindrops

We often draw raindrops as tear-shaped objects. However, raindrops are not really shaped like tears. Actual photographs of raindrops show that they have a number of different shapes. The shape that a raindrop takes depends on how big it is.

Small raindrops are more spherical (round-shaped) than large raindrops. There is a good reason for this. As raindrops fall from the sky, the air presses against them and tends to flatten out the bottoms of the drops. The air rushing past the curved sides of the drops reduces the air pressure on these surfaces, causing them to bulge outward. The larger a drop is, the more the rushing air will cause it to bulge out. Larger drops also fall faster than smaller drops, which causes the drops to bulge even more.

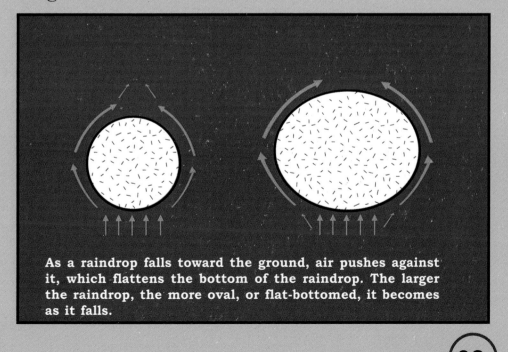

As a raindrop falls toward the ground, air pushes against it, which flattens the bottom of the raindrop. The larger the raindrop, the more oval, or flat-bottomed, it becomes as it falls.

Snow crystals collect on objects whose temperature
is equal to or lower than that of the crystals.

Snow

Even though we would never be able to study each individual snowflake that falls, we know that all snow crystals are hexagons. Hexa- means "six" and -gon means "angle," thus a hexagon is a shape with six angles, or sides. While there are billions of possible forms that ice crystals may take while keeping their basic hexagon shape, all snow crystals that form share distinct shapes.

Snow crystals are silent messengers from the clouds. The size and shape of each crystal indicates the temperature and humidity level within the cloud where the snowflake was formed. Scientists can copy every type of snow crystal in laboratories. They do this by controlling temperature and humidity inside a device called a cold chamber. The tables on the following pages show that temperature seems to have the greatest effect on the shape of snow crystals.

As can be seen, the shape of a snow crystal can

tell us the temperature conditions in the cloud where it was formed. The size of single crystals ranges from about 0.008 inch to about one-half inch in diameter.

As snow crystals fall through clouds, they often bump into each other and stick together. In this way, different-sized snowflakes form. When clouds are thick, the supply of water molecules is high. Because temperatures are near freezing (32°F), snow crystals grow quickly and form fern-like arms. These crystals often clump together and form very large, moist snowflakes. Each flake can contain as many as fifty crystals. The biggest snowflake ever recorded is said to have measured eight inches across! In extremely cold places, such as the North and South Poles, snowfalls tend to be made up of very small, thick, compact crystals.

Snow Crystal Formation

Snow crystals form when super-cooled particles, such as soil and dust from volcanoes drifting in the atmosphere, come into contact with supercooled water

For comparison purposes:

0.13 in. diam.

0.25 in. diam.

0.50 in. diam.

Snow Crystal	Shape	Temperature Range
	Plate	32° F to 26.6° F
	Needle	26.6° F to 23° F
	Hollow plate	23° F to 17.6° F
	Plate	17.6° F to 10.4° F
	Dendrite (stellar)	10.4° F to 3.2° F
	Plate	3.2° F to -13° F
	Hollow columns	-13° F to -58° F

Size in Inches

Plate	.01 to .13
Needle	.25 to .37
Dendrite (stellar)	.03 to .50
Columns	.02 to .13

droplets. Supercooled means that something is colder than freezing temperature but is not yet frozen. The water droplets freeze when they run into the particles, forming snow crystals. You may wonder how scientists know that such particles form snow crystals. The answer is simple. They capture snow crystals, melt them, and then look through a microscope to find the particles around which the crystals had formed. The particles are known as ice nuclei.

Snow Regions

The areas of greatest snowfall in the United States usually lie in the paths followed by winter storms as they travel east across the country. The East Coast of the United States often gets heavy snowfall. So do the areas around the Great Lakes. These parts of the country get so much snow because the warm, moist air from the Gulf of Mexico and the Great Lakes meets with cold air from Canada. When warm, moist tropical air runs into cold, arctic air, snow is the result.

Heavy snowfalls are common in the mountains of the western United States. For example, in parts of Washington, California, Oregon, and Colorado, the average yearly snowfalls are 200 inches. In

Twin Snowflakes?

People often say: "No two snowflakes are alike." This is difficult to understand when we take into account the number of snowflakes that fall in one storm—countless trillions! It does make sense though, since there are billions and billions of possible forms that ice crystals can take while keeping their basic hexagonal shape.

The old saying that no two snowflakes are alike recently seems to have been proven false, however. Nancy Knight, of the National Center for Atmospheric Research, while doing a cloud physics study in 1988, did indeed find two identical snowflakes!

Snowstorm Danger!

Many people enjoy the beauty of freshly fallen snow. When heavy snowfalls occur, however, they can be a serious threat to life and property. In January 1996 a powerful storm hit the East Coast of the United States. As much as two feet of snow piled up in New York City. Record snowfalls were also recorded in Pennsylvania, New Jersey, and West Virginia. Later that month, a rapid thaw quickly melted the snow, causing major river flooding in the entire area. The blizzard, along with the flooding, caused 187 deaths and nearly 3 billion dollars in damage and snow removal costs.

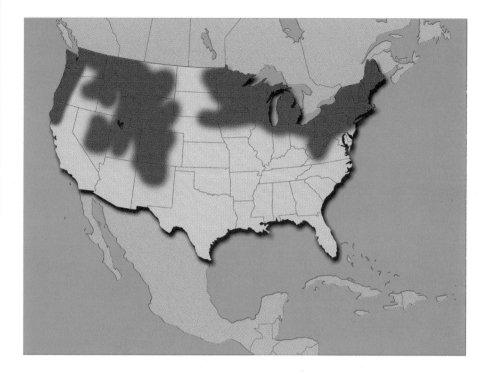

The dark areas on this map show areas of the United States where heavy snowfall is likely to occur.

some mountain areas, the amount of snow that falls is amazing. For example, at Yosemite Park, in California, 450 inches (38 feet) of snow were recorded in one year alone. And at Summit, California, about 100 years ago, nearly 800 inches (66 feet) of snow fell in one winter!

Stranded!

Many people have become stranded in the Rocky Mountains because the snow was too deep to move through. Even powerful trains have gotten stuck. In 1952 a passenger train called the City of San Francisco was caught in a snowstorm as it traveled west through the mountains. The snow piled up so high that powerful diesel engines could not pull the cars through it. Aboard the stranded train were 226 passengers. It took four days for snowplows to reach the stranded people and rescue them.

Some snowfalls are heavy enough to stop a train, like the westward-bound City of San Francisco.

Heavy snowfall occurs in mountain areas for two reasons:

- ⊙ High areas are usually colder than areas near sea level.
- ⊙ Mountains force air masses to move up over their steep sides.

This upward movement causes the air to reach the dew point, and clouds form. In the cold atmosphere of the high mountains, the clouds then release their moisture as snow.

Snow and Glaciers

Glaciers are large rivers of compacted snow. A glacier will form in an area that gets heavy snowfall and where temperatures are cold year round. Since the snow cannot melt, it piles up and sinks under its own weight. Eventually it compacts into ice because of such a huge weight. There are glaciers all over the mountainous areas of the world. Even Africa, with its hot climate, is home to a glacier. Mount Kenya, which is just 200 miles south of the equator, has a large glacier on its peak. Oddly enough, the moisture that feeds the Kenya glacier comes from the steaming rain forests of the jungles below.

Backyard Weather Watcher

We may not like the weather some days, but we have no choice how it is outside. You may choose to stay indoors to fight the effects of weather, but more likely, you will have to go outside every day of the year. Since you must, why not know about weather and understand why it's hot or cold one day, and raining or snowing the next? Why not understand the different cloud types and what their appearance in the sky means?

This knowledge may just help you to think of weather as something more than just "good" or "bad." Weather is vital to our planet. It is something to be enjoyed on a warm summer day. When it rains, though, we must be cautious. So when you look out the window and find thunderheads building on the horizon, you will know why it is going to rain and how that rain formed.

Glossary

acid rain Rain containing high levels of sulfuric or nitric acid. This is created by exhaust from automobiles and factories.

altocumulus lenticularis A lens-shaped cloud that has the appearance of a UFO.

cirrus High, thin, wispy clouds made of ice crystals.

condensation The process in which water changes from a gas to a liquid.

condensation nuclei Any solid surface on which condensation can collect.

cumuliform A category of low, puffy clouds that form vertically.

cumulonimbus Puffy, gray clouds that form vertically and usually produce storms, often called thunderheads.

dew point The point at which the air temperature allows condensation to begin.

drought An extended period of dry weather that may cause serious harm to the environment.

evaporation The process by which a liquid transforms into a gas.

expansion An air-cooling process where clouds are formed when air moves upward in the atmosphere.

humidity The amount of water that is in the air.

kinetic energy The energy of objects in motion, such as that of water vapor molecules.

molecule The smallest part of a substance.

precipitation Any kind of water that falls to Earth, such as rain, snow, and sleet.

saturated Being full of moisture.

stratiform Low, flat clouds.

supercooled Colder than freezing temperature (32° F) without being frozen.

water cycle The process of water evaporating into the air, forming clouds, and having precipitation return to Earth.

water vapor Water in the form of a gas.

upcurrents Winds blowing upward from beneath clouds that hold cloud droplets in the air.

For Further Reading

Abbott, Marti and Betty J. Polk. *Clouds, Rain, Wind and Snow.* Columbus, OH: Fearon Teacher Aids, 1996.

Allaby, Michael. *How the Weather Works.* New York: Readers' Digest, 1995.

Day, John, and Vincent Schaefer. *Clouds and Weather* (Peterson First Guides). New York: Houghton Mifflin, 1997.

Kahl, Jonathan. *Wet Weather: Rain Showers and Snowfall.* Minneapolis: Lerner Publications, 1992.

Kerrod, Robin and J.W. Wright. *Weather (Learn About Series).* New York: Lorenz Books, 1997.

Lehr, Paul, R. Will Burnett and Herbert Zim. *Weather: Air Masses, Clouds, Rainfall, Storms, Weather Maps, Climate.* New York: Golden Books, 1987.

Ludlum, David M., Richard A. Keen, and Ron Holle. *Clouds and Storms* (National Audubon Society *Pocket Guides*). New York: Knopf, 1995.

Rubin, Louis D. and Jim Duncan. *The Weather Wizard's Cloud Book. How You Can Forecast the Weather Accurately and Easily by Reading the Clouds.* Carrboro, NC: Algonquin Books, 1989.

Simon, Seymour. *Weather.* New York: William Morrow, 1993.

Resources

Nick Walker: "The Weather Dude"
P.O. Box 9535
Seattle, WA 98109
Web site: http://www.nwlink.com/~wxdude/
e-mail: wxdude@nwlink.com
KSTW-TV weather forecaster helps kids learn about weather
   and meteorology.

Weather Education and Resources
National Weather Service Office, Portland, Oregon
5241 NE 122nd Avenue
Portland, OR 97230
(503) 261-9246
Web site: http://www.wrh.noaa.gov/portland/educate.html

WEB SITES

Dan's Wild Weather Page
Chief Meteorologist Dan Satterfield, Newschannel 19,
   WHNT-TV Huntsville, Alabama
Interactive weather page for kids
Web site: http://www.whnt19.com/kidwx
e-mail: webmaster@whnt19.com

Weather for Teachers and Kids
Helpful weather-related links for teachers and students.
Web site:
   http://info.abrfc.noaa.gov/wfodocs/weather_kids.html

Index

A
Africa, 40

air, 4, 8, 9, 10, 12, 13, 14, 16, 18, 23, 24, 25, 29
air masses, tropical, 19, 34
air pressure, 16, 29
arctic air, 34
Atlantic Ocean, 13
atmosphere, 4, 8, 9, 10, 13, 14, 16, 17, 18, 20, 28, 32, 34
atmospheric pressure, 16

C
Canada, 34
clouds, types of, 17-21
    cirrus, 17, 20
    cumuliform, 17-18
    cumulonimbus, 18
cumulus, 17, 18, 24, 25, 28
stratiform, 17, 19
stratus, 19, 24, 25
thunderheads, 18, 41
condensation, 10, 12, 23
condensation nuclei, 12, 13, 14, 16, 28
crops, 23, 24

D
deserts, 11, 12
dew point, 12, 16, 18, 40
droughts, 24
dust bowl, 23

E
Earth, 4, 8, 13, 14, 23, 28
energy, 8
equator, 40
evaporation, 9, 10, 14, 18, 23
expansion, 16

F
force, 16, 18
freezing, 20, 28, 32, 34

G
gas, 7, 8
glaciers, 40
Great Lakes, 34
Great Plains, 23, 24
Gulf of Mexico, 13, 18, 34

H
humidity, 11, 12, 31

I
ice, 7, 17, 20
ice crystals, 28, 31
ice nuclei, 34

K
kinetic energy, 9

L
liquid, 7, 28

M
moisture, 8, 10, 12, 13, 23, 40
mountains, 34, 40

N
North Pole, 32

O
ocean, 9, 14

P
Pacific Ocean, 13
particles, 7, 12, 13, 14, 28, 32, 34
plants, 5, 23
precipitation, 5, 11, 23, 24

R
raindrops, 25, 28, 29
rain forests, tropical, 11, 40

S
saturated, 13
sea level, 40
sea salts, 14, 28
sky, 4, 7, 17, 19, 20, 29, 41
snowflake, 31, 32
snow crystals, 31, 32, 34
solid, 7

South Pole, 32
stratosphere, 18
sun, 9, 18
supercooled, 32

T
temperature, 12, 13, 16, 28, 31, 32, 34, 40
thunderstorms, 7, 8

U
United States, 34
upcurrents, 25, 28

W
water, 5, 7, 10, 14, 23, 28, 32, 34
water cycle, 23
water molecules, 9, 10, 32
water vapor, 7, 8, 10, 11, 12, 13, 16, 20, 28
weather, 4, 8, 20, 41
wind, 7, 8, 24, 25, 28

Credits

About the Author
Dean Galiano is a freelance writer. He lives in New York City.

Photo Credits
Cover and Title Page © Digital Stock; p.5 © Galen Rowell/Corbis; pp.6-7 © Cliff Reidinger/Midwestock; p.8 © Jack Zehr/FPG; p.11 © Josef Beck/FPG; p.11 © Corbis; p.15 © Ernst Haas/Tony Stone; p. 17 © W.P. Whitman Photography; p.19 © Eric Gilbert, Papilio/Corbis; p.20,21 © Frank Alexandrowic/ Unifoto; pp.22-23 © Frederick McKinney/FPG; p.24 ©Corbis; p.25 © Larry West/FPG; pp.26-27 © Hulton Getty/Tony Stone; pp.30-31 ©Martha Cooper/Viesti Associates; p.35 ©IBL/The Viesti Collection; p.36 © Caroline Wood/International Stock; pp.38-39 © Corbis/Bettman; pp.10, 14, 16, 29, 32, 33, 37 Illustrations by Lisa Quattlebaum.

Cover Design
Kim M. Sonsky

Book Design and Layout
Lisa Quattlebaum

Consulting Editors
Mark Beyer and Jennifer Ceaser